Making Tracks

Ian Harding

Copyright © 2016 by Ian Harding

All rights reserved. No part of this publication may be reproduced, stored in a retrieval system, or transmitted, in any form or by any means, electronic, mechanical, photocopying recording or otherwise without the prior written permission of the author and the publisher.

CONTENTS

SONNETS	1
Tracks	2
Canvas	3
Remember	4
No Place To Be	5
The Shallows	6
Don't Mention Love	7
The Mind Trails	8
Yesteryear	9
Listen	10
Out There	11
Missing You	12
Rebirth	13
Closure	14
OBSERVATIONS	15

A Flower	16
A Thirsting	17
Fossil	18
The Watcher	19
Past Is Present	20
Sign Posts	21
The Street Bench	22
A Boys Own View	23
Time	24
Casualties	25
Other End	26
...And Then	27
Things In Places	28
Shoreline	29
A Picture	30
The Lost Shoe	31
Revival	32

Humbled	**33**
Echoes	**34**
Life Thought	**35**
Time Out	**36**
Orwellian Last Post	**37**
Consuming	**38**
Lights Out	**39**
Statement	**40**
Consequence	**41**
Me Shadow	**42**
Torrent	**43**
Not Heard	**44**
Bound	**45**
The Distant Critic	**46**
Shadows	**47**
Watch Out People!	**48**
See Saw	**49**

In Your Face	**50**
A Question	**51**
Wake Up!	**52**
The Very Fear	**53**
Last Stand	**54**
Occlusion	**55**
Doors	**56**
I Don't Get It!	**57**
Same Old Lies	**58**
Realisation	**59**
Swan Song	**60**
Observe	**61**
Future Verse	**62**
HUMOUR	**63**
Dismissing Indifference	**64**
A.N. Other	**65**
The Cobbler	**66**

Maiden Flight	**67**
At It	**68**
Retirement!	**69**
Age Concern	**70**
Get Me That….	**71**
Easily Tempted	**72**
Stating The Obvious	**73**
Twang!	**74**
Off The Scale	**75**
EMOTIONS	**76**
A New Beginning	**77**
Delight	**78**
But What About Me?	**79**
Discarded	**80**
Black And White	**81**
Deluge	**82**
The Forgotten Heart	**83**

Lost	**84**
Procession	**85**
Resolve	**86**
Where Am I?	**87**
Dementia	**88**
Over Time	**89**
Neglect	**90**
Unsung Heart	**91**
Hidden	**92**
Sentenced	**93**
Searching	**94**
So It's All Gone?	**95**
Self Portrait	**96**
Loving	**97**
Enchanted	**98**
The Wrong Path	**99**

NATURE   101

Bluebells	**102**
A Thought Planted	**103**
The Park	**104**
Fellows	**105**
Rings Of Truth	**106**
New Horizons	**107**
Spring Day	**108**
April Fresh	**109**
Day Break	**110**
The Spreading Sky	**111**
Summer's View	**112**
Canopy Of Life	**113**
Late Summer's Spectacle	**114**
Spring Forth	**116**
Rain Drops	**117**
After Rain	**118**
The Happening	**119**

Another Leaf Falls	**120**
Curtain Falls	**121**
Autumn Burst	**122**
Winters Grip	**123**
The Forgotten Trees	**124**
Winters Breath	**125**
Abstract Reflections	**126**
Lago Di Como	**127**
Dancing Olives	**128**
Amelia	**129**
Monferrato	**130**
Bearing Witness	**131**
Oceans Wave	**132**
Blue	**133**
Fractus	**134**
The Wave Cloud	**135**
An End to Begin	**136**

Sonnets

Tracks

It finally dawned
That whatever I said
Would not translate,
As I had loved
A language misunderstood.
So they are discarded –
Those marks of joy
The blind falsehoods
Which could not face
Evermore drifting sorrow.
Time erases bygone days
No impressions remain
Just an opening –
Making new tracks.

Canvas

If I drew myself into a painting
How would the world appear
In landscape, in portrait,
In acrylic, oil or watercolour?
Would I sense movement
Marvel over spectrum
Feel aching passion in a
Harbour of wayward thoughts?
Could I express beauty, love and sentiment
Or create a theatre of mystery
Conducting watchful eyes to a symphony
Of confusion or enthrallment?
How would it feel to be a moving creation
That speaks to a several world?

Remember

If I could wish to remember
Then I would recollect
All that fine detail of the original hour.
For to relive the first budding smile
And feel the fair touch of hands
That sparked the rush of loves purpose
To just know in an instant
That that was the day of days in concert
Which would ebb and flow
As the moons tides kissed the wanton shore.
And if by chance I had placed a hand
Before the winds of time
Would it have so captured a fine tomorrow
Or just repeated a reminisce of the day…

No Place To Be

Come to me my love
As though all that was past
Had had no consequence
No place to be
A time that was not
Where you had walked
Unaware of my presence
A mind traversing broken paths
A heart laboring through
A wilderness of hurt
As the sun rises and so falls
Your troubled soul breaches
Hopes broken shore
For the life within takes a step.

The Shallows

I walked in the shallows
Of the land that drew me
As a flush of seasons new
Engulfed my limitless mind –
From there, a flotilla of stars
Dispersed from the still of a pond
Raised my heart to the heavens
From a bed full of fledgling dreams.
So here to my waking moment
I triumphed with resolve –
For to be touched by love
Is a far better fate, than to receive
All the riches of the world
Sprinkled at ones aching feet.

Don't Mention Love

So tell me dear friend
With whom I have vested so much
Why must our loving birth
Be jettisoned through fear?
Are our hearts so fragile
Our minds so weak
That our bodies should flounder
And our dreams fade?
Perhaps we are what we are
Despite of ourselves, so
Dare not speak of love
That never told can be
As without a firm resolve
Those winds do carry away!

The Mind Trails

The thought of you
Trailed in the breeze...
And so I was mindful of you
Upon that very hour -
That I was given
That I was blessed
That I was beautiful
In the arms
Of you a stranger
Indeed upon that very hour -
That I was, as one
That I was that love
That dare not speak its name
That I was, no dream.

Yesteryear

Blossom scatters across
The garden of my mind
Streams of wind play
Around bandstand memories
Of a spring fair
The flutter of bunting
And raucous merriment
Overgrown paths losing definition
Colours dancing to fade off.
Times long past, image
Through stills of smiling faces
A carousel dream state
Piecing together cherished fragments
Of memory to life.

Listen

Listen, listen, listen...
We breathe it, feel it, hear it
In the breeze, in verse
Through cleansing water
To the Sun's healing rays.
It is something that caresses our souls
Not just revered as a fleeting prize.
Then why do our hearts call out
For our heads to destroy?
What is the word we fear
To reject with stop sign hands
Whilst turning towards oblivion?
All we have is here and now...
Listen, listen, listen...

Out There

When was it I noticed, that
Time had moved its path
Its pattern, its meaning
And found one extricated
From the Sun bringing cheer
To the life giving rains
And the pronouncing winds of change.
I could sense life, see its purpose
Yet it could not witness me.
No breath, no sound
Nothingness causing thought –
Outside of being.
Was I knocking, as I could not hear
Through the din of angels weeping.

Missing You

I miss you –
For the heart that sings.
I miss you –
For the soul that bares.
I miss you –
For the inner strength that shines.
I miss you –
For the beauty that you possess.
I miss you –
For the humility that you show.
I miss you –
For the love that hides within.
I miss you –
For the joy of just missing, you.

Rebirth

I know little of sense
Even less of love
Yet my soul searches, searches
Fulfilment of my heart.
In mirrors you call
I stare, wondering –
Wandering through time
Confused with hope.
Your light comes and goes
Yet I must not judge –
As healing is growth.
For it is a reborn life
Facing the mirrors, that
Will love me back true.

Closure

The room was full of you, and yet
You would not ever enter again.
You were a silent ending
Threaded into a mist of memory.
I could not believe you were gone
No! You must still be there, because
If I were to turn my head, I would know
That your sweet eyes would kiss my dream
And we would walk again hand in hand.
The transposition confounds me, as
I am lost in your secret world
With no hope of being discovered.
I had you but I have you no more
The curtains were drawn to a close.

Observations

A Flower

So what's in a flower?

Is it the face of perception or...
The beauty of display?

Is it the scent of an angel or...
The innocence of bloom?

Is it for love or...
The tears of sorrow?

Is it the truth that...
Dares not wish to speak?

So what's in a flower?

A Thirsting

Across the ever stretching sky
Beckons an oasis of words
Sprinkled with abundant letters
That invites a journeys tale.
Though the sands of time
Tread deep and slow
Those overreaching branches
Display promises of future verse.

Fossil

A single breath
Freshens a fingerprint
Etched to a window pane
An evanescent fossil found
Of unimaginable depth
Breathing out to future generations
That will rediscover transparency.

The Watcher

I watched the mirror
At the start of day
And at its close
Each surfacing moment
Proffered change
Sometimes imperceptibly
But nevertheless change
Seemingly, everything caught
By its gaze, aged
But the mirror itself
Recording dances of age
Promised play and pause
With the minds eye.
In time the watcher
Accepted natures pleasure
We arrive as frail infants
Cavort as naive children
Love and stress as adults
All to end our days again
In child like reflection
Pulling faces back at the watcher.

Past Is Present

How narrow the world is
You are known and loved
For an age, yet forgotten
When the sun rises -
Though, in an instant
A smell, a word
Jolts the conscience
Releases memory, a vision
That will hold the head
Until the sun bows.

Sign Posts

Life, full of sign posts
For us to follow

Some, to engage us
Others, to confuse

Do we blindly tread as others do
Or question, be it mad or true

Is the direction quietly sound
Or do we take the detour around.

The Street Bench

The street bench
So often passed by
Offers too many
A moment of rest
A place of sanctuary
A time to reflect
A mind set to think
A pause to consider.

The street bench
So often missed
Offers too many
A moment to hug
A place to talk
A time to meet
A mind set to smile
A pause without fanfare.

Our street bench
So often witnessed
Offers too few
A brass plated memory
A hearts imprint
A graffiti statement
A birds perch
A passing history.

A Boys Own View

I call out for yesteryear days
So much time, so many plays
The freedom to bicycle far and wide
Even as far as the sea to chase the tide

To keep in Mums good books for many a day
So Dad would willingly hand out pocket money pay
A three penny bit, tanner or even a mere penny
Would serve sufficient to choose sweets a many

Sherbert dips, pear drops and jamboree bags
Or masses of black jacks and fruit salads enough to brag
So much for so little for me, me, me!
My stash to dip into with utmost glee

Family outings and holidays along England's coasts
Staying in guest houses and having Sunday roasts
Flip flops, ice creams, buckets and spades
What fun to be had with parents trapped in shades.

Time

What is time, if
One day is full, and
The next spent
Without thought.

Where is time, when
You cry out for more, or
Strive to regain
Without faltering.

Why is time, a
Wonderful friend, yet
An unwanted pursuer
Without sensibility.

Will, this time
Enrich our lives, or
Wander aimlessly
Without recoil.

Casualties

Dark rivers of tormented tarmac
Sentineled by serpent headed lights
Submit to stressed human cargo
Travelling to destinations far and wide.
To reaching signs and broken lines
A never ending telegraph tide
Flowing with the sparkle of feral eyes
Onward bound with no compromise.
Casualties decorate the bleak roadside
A constant wake of wasted feather and fur
Except for the scavenging carrion fights
Of magpies, rooks and crows
Squawking with utter delight!

Other End

I have often wondered
What is meant by the
Other end of the spectrum.
Is it just a logical end or
Does a voyage begin?
Would it be to a world of unknowns
Looking outside in, inside out
Or is there another end
At the end
And to what end?
I have often wondered...

...And Then

...and then I worried
and marched
and voiced
and then, did nothing!

...and then I accepted
and did not march
and did not voice
and then, did not think to worry!

Things In Places

I like to place things in places
That catch the eye
That set a mood
That halt a step

I like things, because they are not
Caught up in verbiage
Or the written word
But just shout a presence

Places without things pass the eye
Dull the world
Address nothingness
So just a void.

Shoreline

I walk in solitude
At the waters edge, except for
The wind asserting its presence
Showering misty bouquets of smell.
The relentless drive of the sea
Adds a measure of seasoning
Pummelling hidden secrets
As the tide recedes graciously
In deference to the moon.

A world of stories unfold
Of both loss and discovery
A length of driftwood alights the shore
Scarred and broken, perchance
Released from a mariners grave?
And a mermaids kiss stone, lost to
A past storm, releases its charm.
I sense onward souls
Calling from afar…….find me!

A Picture

I saw this man sitting
On the edge of a sand dune
Staring out to the sequined sea
Perchance in his field of vision
Some twenty feet away and no more
Sat a newly formed coupling
Amorous to the core.
It seemed strangely odd
That neither he nor they
Were in anyway accepting or even aware
To the closeness of positioning
But relished containment of their own horizon
To the omission of all.
Beauty of lost thought
And the wonder of new love
Were together all embracing.

The Lost Shoe

I find it strangely odd
That a day does not pass, without
Witnessing the loss of a shoe
No longer to pound astride the other
Just simply banished to the curb side.

Was there ever a foot encased?
Had it tramped far and wide?
Was it polished with pride, or
Simply worn to obliteration?

How odd, it should end its days
In lost isolation, no more
To comfort a foot, or
Indeed to run amok.

The lonely shoe finds solace, as
By the rough roads and pathways
Flounder the single glove, sock and soother
Just as bereft without significant others.

Someone is lamenting over a tragic loss
Reeling from a commanding stand
Or jettisoned through jest
Life's imponderables, so full of odds and ends.

Revival

At the end of a day
With no answers
One is drawn to the thought
Of sensual relaxation
The taps are turned
Lights dimmed
And candles charged
As clothes fall away
With soft musical notes
Cavorting through steaming seahorses
That ride over long forgotten tales.
I have thankfully slipped back
Into a world of possibility.

Humbled

Happy should we be
With time so fair
Never really sparing
Any outward thoughts
To declare, that others
With time so rare
Achieve altogether much
That selfless enrichment
To huge applause
With no crutch.

Echoes

Within four walls
And a sound roof
Whisper echoes of present
That vibrate
In parallel dimension
To those that
Have gone before.
A new understanding
To heal
Resolves misty issues
Of echoes past
That purifies
An aching soul
Within four walls
And a sound roof.

Life Thought

Birthing is to welcome Spring
Living is to indulge Summer
Ageing is to experience Autumn
Remembering is to value Winter.

Time Out

How odd is time itself
You cannot see it
Taste it, smell it
And yet it touches you
It changes you imperceptibly
By the second, minute, hour, day.

If you express something
Here and now
It is already past
And if you think ahead
By the time you've got there
It's gone!

It never sleeps
It just watches, silently
It can be a true friend
Or a sly enemy.

It is always truthful
It never ever lies
So celebrate the odd
As you will never get even.

Orwellian Last Post

Faces awash with shadows
Long eyes grey as nimbostratus
Oppressed minds lost to outer regions
Contained voices as muted bugles

In a world of fading dreams

Bodies with hung shoulders
Hearts of intermittent rhythm
Souls smothered, riches squandered
Heads of un-persons imploding.

Consuming

In resting
It happened
I became
Something to everything
Transfixed in regression
Camouflaged around nature
Blended through
A diaphanous portal.
I touched moving lands
Breathed torrents of surprise
Witnessed unworried beings
Flying transient lives.
Memories flash and fade
I am a shade of this
For a portrayal of that
It would appear, in a world
Wonderfully disorganised
Beautifully orchestrated.

Lights Out

The room of no consequence
Erupts into darkness around
The stunted breath of self
Interweaving with the oddest
Creaks, bumps, car revs and hoots.
So to the night world
Beyond fenestration
Demanding our attention, as clouds
Billow behind structured trees, and
Autumnal street lamps braid sister leaves
Nature possesses you, controls you
Draws the senses, until the
Bright light camouflages back
To the room of no consequence.

Statement

They came for me, those
Teasing words of yester year
Pushing for tomorrow's potential.
The river flowed fast
With a swell of letters
Babbling in confusion
Their music not yet heard
Their melody unable to settle
Their journey unrelenting.
How would I make sense of it all
Where would inspiration manifest
To ever deliver life's profundity?

Consequence

There are moments
I have left with you
That rattle the conscience
Though, not placed by design
Hang as seasonal reminders...
As the wind that chastens
The Sun that scalds
And the rain that lashes
They all leave visual abrasions
For future layers to bond.

Me Shadow

I was once your shadow

I followed you everywhere
I ran when you ran
I tripped when you tripped

I mimicked your every move

I existed because of you
I your alter ego
I me shadow

In a conspiracy of moving shadows.

Torrent

Like a wash
That has not cleansed

Like a closed room
Banished of light

Like an occluded front
Menacing the sky

Like a first frost
Strangling life

Like a presence of you
That deserves nothing!

Not Heard

I am a somebody that I know
Moved by wonders
Breezed through stimuli
A propagation of ripened reveal
For I am a thought indulger
An expression of others exception
The face of the one
The incidental of self
A mirror of reflection
Shouting from a muted voice.

Bound

Dreams of unknowns
Manifest from script
Outing bruised fragments

Reality of knowns
Dissipated through time
Cast out as shadows

Spirit bounded rooms
Cornering every move
Struggling for definition

Repeated memories
Mirror poor reflection
Bidding soul bared.

The Distant Critic

Folly! I heard you say
Standing proud on your sullen soapbox
Lording it and clever with it
Threading negatives over another's dream
But through folds of time
Like the turning pages of a book
Those prophetic words end burning.
Think not how things might have been
For it is plain that all have seen
The true nature of your impious soul
Now driven afar to a different hole.
You are eaten up, spent and hollow
A lost man with no one to follow.

Shadows

Shadows shelter
Or, do they hide

Shadows protect
Or, do they endanger

Shadows mimic
Or, do they play

Shadows distort
Or, do they reflect

Shadows cool
Or, do they cast out?

Watch Out People!

People are people wherever they walk
Gossip mongers, finger pointers, purveyors of blame
Quick to give out, pedestrian when at fault
These tribal tribulations excuse reapers of destruction
And all to win over innocent foraging fellows
Our disconnect bursts open swathes of relentless rain
This is our world in which we walk in shame.

See Saw

I love so therefore I live
I dream so therefore I create
I care so therefore I falter
I need so therefore I strain
I want so therefore I hunger
I desire so therefore I promise
I wonder so therefore I pray
I live so therefore I die.

In Your Face

Life is so sure...
It seems

Life is so now...
It screams!

Life is so here...
It beams

Life so it flows...
It streams...

Away

A Question

What makes me the way I am?
Carved out perhaps by the very hand of God?
Or simply hewn from parental coursing?
Maybe character is moulded through sibling rivalry
Even painfully learnt through playground antics.
Could it have been an early injustice
Fracturing my spirit to follow a certain life groove?
There before me as I simply age is one simple truth
That all things start, progress and end
With me and no other.

Wake Up!

Human kind the ultimate marauder
Walking in deference with other species
Always thirsting for knowledge but understands little
We take and take more not rightfully ours
Arrogances destroy our planet, our souls, our very being
A danger of too many, too much, too often
Will result in a loss too great to fathom
Adaptation and humility must be the battle cry
To maintain supremacy
Time to wake now, before dawn is no more
Harvest a new vision, embrace it
Develop strength in thought and connect
And mans ingenuity will encounter another day.

The Very Fear

Go to the night my friend
With dawn as your defence
Shake off the talons of fear
And de-cloak the night's myth
Walk the steady path
For shadows will flatten
To clear the way.

You are now the shadow
That preys upon the ill prepared
A choking adversarial force
And when your night's work is done
And shed its predatory clothes
You venture in search of natures store
But beware my friend –

As you may just receive, the devils hand!

Last Stand

At first frost
Stubborn leaves
Wave and fall.

Occlusion

Seagull laughing
Child crying
Chips flown!

Doors

Doors are for opening
Doors are for closing
We all close doors

Doors are opened to greet
Doors are slammed to evict
We all slam doors

Doors are kept shut
Doors are kept locked
We all hold the keys!

I Don't Get It!

The day of the match
Adrenalin releases the latch
For pack mentality must fuse
Shirts on, ready to abuse

The pack is heralded by the horn
As the players cuss, hack and warn
The referee struts his stuff
But must distinguish against light rebuff

So called professional players lie and cheat
Desperate in their minds to beat
Sadly so many youngsters learn the craft
Incredulous it seems, altogether daft

The game may be won or lost
But do we know at what cost
Days after, fathers and sons don the club shirt
Only to continue dishing the dirt

This is not the football I crave
Why can't players and supporters behave?
Skilful play is all we should credit
Otherwise, I'm afraid, I just don't get it!

Same Old Lies

Your controlled lips
Spew out controlled words
To control the floor -
For your control
Controls another
To control others -
Through controlled lips
That spew out controlled words
To control.

Realisation

It is not
That I have tried
Or not tried
Or that I have
Failed or won
But that I can
Start something
That will lead
To joyous horizons for
The realisation of a dream.
For out there
Everyone goes about their lives
Some with beacons
Others to do the following
It takes just one
And everyone
For the world to turn
A page of discovery.

Swan Song

Without saying it
You know if pushed
That he would venture to agree
I am a proud man.

Without asking it
You know if concerned
That he would venture to admit
I am a principled man.

Without seeking it
You know if acknowledged
That he would venture to say
I am a kindly man.

Without showcasing it
You know if challenged
That he would venture to risk
I am a man prepared to be open.

Without broadcasting it
You know if questioned
That he would venture to accept
I am a man ready to sleep.

Observe

A dark cloud
Covers a head
But allows
Waving steps.

Future Verse

I danced through
A room of words
Yet nothing was there
At least nothing discernible
Save that for beauty
Of butterfly wings revealing
Glimpse and prospect.
I followed awkwardly as their flight
A meandering generality
Flickering intent over
A colourscade of suitors.
A light breeze motioned
A dance of spiral and kiss
In steady rhythm, circling
Ever closer to full fantasia
And the release of future verse.

Humour

Dismissing Indifference

Sometimes I do
And
Sometimes I don't
It is not for you to reason
But
It is for you to know
I like the way I am
And
I like not the way you are
So please go!

A.N. Other

To the others
Other than myself
I salute one or other farewell
But away from the others
On the other hand
I welcome other new arrivals
Other than the occasional other
I am naturally engaged of the other
Perhaps others will join me
Other than doing something or other
Maybe it is time to choose A.N.OTHER
And if we look the other way
More than likely we will uncover the other
To be the new voice of the others.

The Cobbler

I come with hope –
And a question.
Can you do anything
For my sole mate?
There is a hole
In my life
That needs to be filled.
You're the man
In the white coat
That repairs a-plenty.
No more the broken
Buckle or clasp,
No more the flapping sole
I'll leave your shop
With new laces
And a skip in my step.

Maiden Flight

Stood at the top of my hill today
Breathing the bestest of breaths
Because I could!
Spirit lapping the edge of possibility
For no-one or nothing was there to stop me
I was free to run –
To run as fast as I knew I could
Full pelt down the grass covered hill
Faster and faster and faster
So fast that I stumbled
And ran even faster and faster and faster
I was falling, I gasped, I took off
I was flying!

At It

Everyone's at it!
I can see that!
But what are they doing?
Search me!

Do you think
They appreciate
What they're doing?
I doubt it!

So why are they
Doing it?
Because….
Everyone is!

If that's the case
What's the point
Of doing it?
Good question!

Do you think
We should be
Doing it?
Absolutely yes!

Retirement!

Time for retirement
Nice thought, but just -
Bugger off!

I know it is
My fate to become
A rusting wreck
That no one wants to know
That no one knows what to do with
Except humour perhaps.

I simply do not want
To be greyed out
To be unnoticed
To become one of the forgotten people.

So I will defend my days
I will deny my age
I will destroy the myth
I will dance eternal youth!

Age Concern

We know it's coming
But
We will deny it

We know it's the truth
But
We will hide it

We know it will catch us
But
We will try and avoid it

We know it will
But…

Get Me That….

Get me that…doodah
You know, the doubrey
The oojamaflip
Damn it, you know!

The thinga-mebob
Whats its face
Thingy thing
Oh! Flipping heck, you know!

Watcha-macallit
Howsya father
You know, the whatsit
Oh! Just forget it!

Easily Tempted

No, never!
I couldn't possibly!
Could I?

Perhaps? No!
But, then again -
Why not?

No, seriously!
Must I?
O, go on then!

Stating The Obvious

It's a bit nippy out!
It is bloody winter you know
What do you expect?
Yeah, suppose so.

It's a bit wet out!
It is bloody spring you know
What do you expect?
Yeah, suppose so.

It's a bit hot out!
It is bloody summer you know
What do you expect?
Yeah, suppose so.

It's getting dark out!
It is bloody autumn you know
What do you expect?
Bloody winter again!

Twang!

Tick, tick, tock
Tock, tock, tick
Bong, bong, twang!

Ticking sucks -
Over time!
Tocking great!

Off The Scale

When all around
Is off the scale of reason
Take a step forward

When all around
Is off the scale of good
Take a step back

When all around
Is off the scale of obvious
Walk away

When all around
Is said and done
Dig a hole.

Emotions

A New Beginning

A love far less than mine
Stands truly apart
But the one that is equal
Walks hand in hand
Through a world of in-betweens
As there is never a rush
For the perfect time to arrive.

Delight

We have no endings –
Just sweet beginnings.
So let us relax and drift
Along the paths that kiss
And delight our very souls
Let us promise that our adventure
Will be never ending
And our thoughts as Nature's sweet intent.
I gift to you my smile
As I am bound to accept yours
We are to love, for
Beauty's sake alone.

But What About Me?

I've lost all sense of me
I don't know where it's gone!

I used to get me
But I don't know where I am!

I feel that I should comply
But what about me?

But what about me...
I've lost all sense of me.

Discarded

So…
Throw away your love's song
And…
See where it takes you.
Yes…
I would guess along broken paths
To…
Parade with splintered feet.
Never…
Finding suitors of distinction
Sadly…
Knowing your loss of judgement.
Then…
Remembering love's song discarded
As…
You make lamenting tracks.

Black And White

Where was the girl I loved -
How did the story end?

The landscape slid
Quietly from consciousness

The sun raced across the sky
To the infinite horizon

And her heart cooled
By the moons shore

Everything was black and white
Yet the translation was lost.

Deluge

If it is to rain
Then it should rain.

If it should rain
Then it must rain.

If it must rain
Then let it rain!

The Forgotten Heart

Purest love
Sweetest thorn
My heart tears
With little sound
As smiles within
Clamour cold hope
Through the silence
Of truth searching.

Lost

Where am I?
What has gone wrong?
The dream has slipped
Matter collides with matter
Nothing makes sense
Nothing feels right
The heart bruises all over
The mind filters debris
So want to be loves first thought
So want to picture but cannot see
So confused, so lost!

Procession

Candles burning
Eyes a bright
Onward glowing
Out of sight.

Misty memory
Mind aloof
Lost telemetry
Seeking truth.

Resolve

Shackled –
I reached.

Blinded –
I searched.

Persecuted –
I strived.

Revered –
I conquered.

Where Am I?

I find the world
very confusing these days.
At times
I find myself
in far flung places.
Also amazed to find
my bed street parked
in the middle of the night.
I call out
no one hears.
I suppose
they are all asleep.
Where am I? I ask.
My aged and clever brain
impatient with the body's fall
protects and lavishes
adventures upon me.
Lucidity is actually
hard work you know!
Hurry up!   I must not -
Miss the next train!

Dementia

The marshalling mind
Full of scattered memories
And piled up papers
Shouts in confusion
Arresting thoughts.
For every breath
Blows sense away
And every outreaching
Sets silence splintering
Through the shattering
Of all those known
And safe mirrors.
I am reduced to a nonsense
An unknown sorry simpleton
So I scream everyone's
Darkest nightmare
For no one sees
No one hears
No one remembers
No one!

Over Time

When the love is done
And burnt embers scatter
Remember that each day
Above ground, is a glorious day
As the beauty of time
Becomes your most ardent lover.

Neglect

I thought I was loved –
Until you forgot to kiss.

I thought I was needed –
Until you forgot to look back.

I thought I was your soulmate –
Until you forgot to share.

I thought we were as one –
Until we forgot to dream.

Unsung Heart

Forgive this foolish man, that
Reveals his heart to the elements -
The quiet one that loves from afar
And does not rest his ardour or pursuit.
Though he may not share his opposite reflection
On that to which he truly craves
He must journey discovering that love
In its truest form is there but to serve.
So be present for a cooling heart
And rejoice in its purity of purpose
For there will be days of cheer
With the throng of nature's call.

Hidden

You don't see it -
Until it's gone.

You don't feel it -
Until the heart aches.

You don't hear it -
Until the echo returns -

All that you had cherished.

Sentenced

Above the roofs
Across from the tower
Compassion waits for me
But I am rooted
To where I am
My voice rings out
It falls, mute
To the ground
Tears pound a steady beat
As a condemned man falls.

Searching

Imagine a depth of feeling
That may never be quite achievable

Imagine a story hidden from the world
That may never express a completeness

Imagine a longing to loves truth
That may never show its ardour

Imagine a life without expression
That will never be illuminated

Imagine a creative flair, thwarted
That will never be shared

Imagine a world without vision
That will never witness a new dawn

Imagine this blanket waterfall
That will never shed a single tear.

So It's All Gone?

Not to blow sweet nothings –
So fill the time with practicalities.

Not to laze around in each other's arms –
So plan the next events.

Not to make love –
So just go through the motions.

Not to kiss wave –
So then stare goodbye.

Not to kid ourselves –
So it's all but gone.

Self Portrait

A portrait of self
Slam dunked to the pane
Expresses nothing of note
A world flat lined
One dimensional, flawed
Ostracised to the
Bevel edge of hope
Searching self-expression.

Loving

When I too long have loved you well
As indeed my hearts treasure bears –
That of a rose that would not age.
For you who had lifted my hopeful eyes
To bear witness around the purest of souls
I am truly a fortunate man.
Where rhythms are and where rhythms flow –
As love would have as love would show.

Enchanted

Let me whisper
Love in the breeze
And then you my flower
Will show to please.

The Wrong Path

Look not to my eyes
As a pathway to my soul
For they drift with the wind
To what end
To what beginning
I do not know
But you will be carried
With no destination.

So throw off the deluge of rain
The best is yet to come.

Look not to my heart
As an elixir for life
For it will rise
For it will fall
To conquer
To disappoint
But the warmth will embrace
With no promise.

So throw off the deluge of rain
The best is yet to come.

Look not to my words
As a testament of truth
For they arrive entangled
With no clear intent
With no foundation
To hold firm
But the verse will entice
With no refrain.

So throw off the deluge of rain
The best is yet to come...

Nature

Bluebells

It was in the walk of the woods
That I happened upon a vision
-a vision that caught a rush of wind
That laughed around my human form –
A moments distraction
As shards of sun tore through the canopy.
For there, emblazoned before my eyes
Blew a triumphant chorus of bluebells
That rang out their exalted praise
To their Maker's visionary eye.

A Thought Planted

I step outside of self
Harbouring a notion, to
Plant a thought, for
Ahead lies a square metre
Of good productive earth
The ground heaves
Encouraging implant
I hesitate, dream struck
To the enormity, that is
Future growth.

My precious thought
Would root, would rise
With ambition to branch
To blossom, to produce
Fresh thoughts for
A new generation.
Should I stay and tend
Or slip back into self
And let the world discover
A thought well dug?

The Park

The open space calls
For time to slow
As the light breeze plays
By a crowd of fashioned trees.
Breaking strands of warm Sun
Awake the child within
The collective missions
Of local folk unfold.
An old man topples along
As does a child chasing its first ball
Competitive horse play abounds
Within the same fragmented air
Of new lovers melting and
Old friends colluding in laughter.
The Parks nature stands resolute
To the carnival spirit that pervades
Just for a short while but leaving
Its trace of disrespectful debris
As the bowing Sun retreats.

Fellows

It is said
At the grand gathering of trees
That wisdom shall and must flow
From medium to medium.
Fellows of the Institution of Trees
Will sacrifice their rings of learning
Embracing life from life.
You will be revered
By hundreds, thousands, perhaps millions
And your birthplace
Will be thus known as Library.
Take heed my fellow trees
Some of you will survive
For generations to come!

Rings Of Truth

I stand before you -
Proud and waving

I stand aloft of you –
Majestic and strong

I stand around you –
Breathing and growing

I stand after you –
Peaceful and wise.

New Horizons

As waters course
So beauty expresses
By its flow
Constancy builds
So must its anger
Swell to bursting
Seeking new horizons
Awaiting alluvial kiss.

Spring Day

The first beautiful Spring day
Awakens deep dormant desires
Compelling the soul to run
Engage with, enthuse, embrace
Around and around, over and over again.
So blissfully exhilarating
I flounder over the
Grass deck of daisy'd passion -
Taking on a contemplative pose
Drawing on a patchwork quilt
Of blues, whites and greys
Caressed by fresh warm breezes
Teasing me to a sense of adventure….

April Fresh

O for the joys of Spring, the
Twittering call of Robins, the
Haunting coo-cooing of wood pigeons
The sound of brook water racing.

Leaves forcing through a show, of
Life from dull dormant timbers, thrilling
The spirit with rapturous applause, as
They unfold their breathing bounty.

Trees steal early limelight
By a delicate display of long
Awaited colour and fragrance
To be thrown to the winds
Decorating gardens and minds.

A floral tribute follows
Like a weddings fantasia
With fresh droplets of liquid sunshine
Sprinkling diamonds in our eyes.

Day Break

The day begins like so many
A little delicate yet sampling
As to what should be done.

A strong play emerges from cover
As Spring arrives with her attendant rains
Teaming together like invading infantry
Across the gridded sky of battle
With clouds moving fearlessly forward
Mounted high as proud chess pieces.

The scene is wild and fractious
As great flashes of white steel
Consort to destroy and taunt
Catapulting innocents into the
Orchestral passion of battle.

The final furore is served
Clinically by the Sun's command
Prizing open shafts of triumphant rays
Forcing falling rains to disperse and hide.

The day ends like so many
A little delicate yet sampling
As to what should be done.

The Spreading Sky

I look towards the spreading sky
My open portal to ascend and fly
To blow upon lazy flocculent clouds
I feel so free away from the crowds
So high above the earth beneath
If only I could capture this beauty to bequeath.

Summer's View

There in view is a Summer's day
That blows sweet kisses of warmth
Over the scanning eye witnessing
Nature's lucripetous hunger.

The Summer sky, a highway of intricacy
Showcases seeds with flights of fancy
Multitudes of insects darting, floating, buzzing
Throngs of birds nesting, singing out for joy.

The glistening flash of still ponds
Invites a multiplicity of flickers and dance
Pond hoppers deftly beat rhythmic ripples
Whilst courting dragonflies kiss and glide.

Flowers dance to the warm breeze
The season's kaleidoscope of sheer delight
Summer's view is in full swing
With nothing wishing to hide.

Canopy Of Life

O how we marvel
The rebirth of green
Bringing new life
Embracing a fresh breeze

O how we marvel
The full canopy displayed
Full up of life
Demanding our embrace

O how we marvel
The golden glow
With the majesty of release
And the peaceful repose

O how we marvel
At the strength in sleep
Hidden from view
Breathless! Waiting to please.

Late Summer's Spectacle

The sense of relax slowly reveals
As the suns beams press down
The mind allows dreamy escape
Registering a symphonic sequence of sounds
That pleasures the winds, as they
Brush and comb the grateful derma.

Above, jet streams write graffiti
Criss-crossing with outlandish kisses
As swifts and swallows harvest the sky
In salvos of screams
Whilst blackbirds bicker
A metronome of agitation

The sounds of early evening, provide
A monumental experience of clarity
With waves of delectable harmonies
Drawing in the ebbing day
As the air is filled with cavorting clouds
Of aromatic fragrance, that
Sail on the evening breeze.

The smell of barbeque coals and food
And cutlery pinking on plates
Accompanied by a mix of altercations and laughter
Completes the late Summer's afternoon spectacle
As the strands of sun
The last remaining gift of the day
Teases behind fashioned trees.

Spring Forth

The un-rush of Spring
Signals its joy per diem
From the aristocratic arrival
Of pure snowdrops, whispering
To courtiers of crocuses -
In turn, to make way
For the trumpeting daffodils
And the trees confetti of celebration.
Bursting leaves like playful children
So adorn solid dependable bark
Spirits drawn from Mother Earth.

How I long to free fall
With natures determined deluge
The pure notes and discords
Wonderfully agitating bio rhythms
Within a globe of intrigue and discovery
A butterfly kisses the air in flight
As a leaf falls ungraciously to ground
A roaming seed teases its followers
And birds broadcast the days delight
For everything is purposeful
To fashion sense from hidden clues.

Rain Drops

We have commenced
We wish to be heard
You will listen and listen well
We will tap at first
Like playful children
And progress to
An annoying drumming
Until we have your attention!
We require your respect
As much as the beating Sun
We are liquid sunshine
We are life givers
We are beautiful!

After Rain

Weighted leaves bow to passing rains
Must vegetation salutes the senses
Mottled lichen swells with delight
Unassuming threaded veins gorge liquid life
Invisible growth spans in orchestral symphony
Of beauty, dance and bouquet
Accentuating a richness of harvest
As the Sun star sprinkles its diamonds.

The Happening

A leaf falls, trembling
To the uninvited
Ground swell of spent life
Though far from resting
In layered blaze
A radiant fusion stirs
A regenerative throng
Bursting for a new happening.

Another Leaf Falls

A leaf turns
Another leaf falls
Their seasons past
Their greens tinged
With rusting fires
That blow away
Their gasping beauty.

One last shimmering shake
Leaves dormant timbers
Full of spirited sap
Awaiting the kiss
Of natures breath
To reshow its revelation
Before a leaf turns
And another leaf falls.

Curtain Falls

Autumn, the alter ego
Of spirited spring days
Stains green pleasures
For nature dares to discard
As the curtain must fall.

The wrapping wind
A worthy adversarial friend
Battles through webs of bark
Searching out the last lingering leaf
For the curtain has fallen.

Time enough for reflective thought
Such wondrous days were had
So many dreams spawned, though
For every final curtain that falls
An encore will be demanded.

Autumn Burst

An autumn rush of glowing leaf
Thrust out from blackened bark
With raucous ravens and rooks
Serves notice well of winters brief

The sunken sun hides in the hills
Whose job is done and more
As mass celebration harvests
All over another vintage year

Sleep well my lands
With hidden store
Bide this time with careful hands
Until your time comes again to roar.

Winters Grip

An icy blow from the frozen waste
Challenges all to wrap up and make haste
Trees now caught in shocked white
Shadowing fields through winters might

The stark morn not welcomed by all
Heralds the grace of the seasons call
We exist in the mode of complain
Gripped by the boldness of winters domain.

The Forgotten Trees

Trees suffer humiliation of yearly winter
Stripped of green pleasure focals
The starkness borders abandonment
Shuddering to deathly silence
There is barely a fleeting glance
From the once ardent admirer.

The contained stillness of the night
Cooled by the moons glowing beams
Reminds cold grey matter, of
Forgotten beauty that will once again
Slap our joyful faces with wonder
As nature commands our full commune.

Winters Breath

A breath of cold air
Ravages the lungs
A crow laughs haughtily
From a nearby branch
A deer appears unexpectedly
As a jack rabbit races
The grooved barren land.
A hawk holds steady
With its fearsome scoped eyes
Natures hand takes hold
The shroud of silence
Becomes deafening
Under the speckled rose sky -
All is to change fleetingly
Before the picture resettles.

Abstract Reflections

The distorted picture, of
Real life settles on windows
Shapely leaves are lost in blur
As reaching trees search for definition.

Jets dart across the pane, in
Somewhat angular guise.
Trails stretch like elongated clouds
Colours of flowers dull, as
Though pressed in books.

Ornamental features serve, to
Hint at a different world
Even people seem to float by
In a parallel, but
Untouchable domain.

Lago Di Como

Lords rise from still water -
Clouds skirt their dutiful reverence.
Ferry's broadcast in cello modus –
Strumming through silver ripples.
Human flock arrives in season -
Irritating around washed edges.
There is beautiful song –
The horizon never changes its melody.
Only dreams will ebb and flow –
Around the statement clink of glass.

Dancing Olives

Olive tree platoons
Stand to order
Trunks bent and twisted
Dancing waltzes around
Collective gesticulations.
Such uplifting canopies
Facing elements unkempt
Yet green blood courses
Fruit presenting at
The end of century's season.

Amelia

A settled landscape
Of silent whisper
Teases out
Long forgotten tales;
For Cyprus trees
Entrenched like sentinels
Watch over
Green blooded olive groves.
Mountains rise, in
Backdrop sequence,
Supporting white stone citadels
Of generational patents.
An orange hew of evening
Dresses the land, through
Scorched harvests, and
Roasted terracotta roofs
As crickets clatter air waves
Loudly above amorous Latin calls.

Monferrato

Amid the sun's rays
Glimpsing through mist
Stands the spire
Of Monferrato
It's earthen bricks
Of terracotta splay
Invite a warmth
Drawn from the heart
Through italics of time
Etched for permanence
Reminding us of our own
Transient flight.

Bearing Witness

I am the king of the skies
With effortless glide to hold
Edging thermals and winds with cries
For lost reflective souls.
Bearing witness to massing gales
That bully the flight of clouds
With cold blues to winded sails
Rolling, surging all the while.
For those elements of sun, sea and sky
Will battle time and time again
In frenzied fashion to vie
For the hearts and minds of men.
I have soared to great heights
I have conquered many lows
I have fought with all my might
I have witnessed all that nature shows.

Oceans Wave

The oceans wave audibly
As proud shoulders exalt
In triumphant smiles
The indifference of the deep
That inspires our world -
For humility presents
A vast roll that rumbles
A spirit to witness
Adventurers shroud lifted -
To the joy of daring
The reach of unknowns
And the deliverance of new realms
So beguiling the oceans wave.

Blue

On the subject of blue
Be it the sky of heavens
Or the wave of oceans
Go the dreams of man.
The beautiful blue discovery
The one spectral colour of seven
That inspires warmth from cold
Invites the pathfinder of hope -
For beyond the cloak of azure
And the belt of the abyss
Venture countless stories untold
But those elements of blue
Serve up many a contradiction.

Fractus

A cotton belt of Cumulus
Rubs up to the ever so Cirrus
To mock the O so grey Nimbostratus.
The flotilla collaborates
To disband the mottled gloom
And so release the beauty of Nacreous.

The Wave Cloud

A maverick cloud, am I
Out there on my own
Conspicuous in flight
With a backdrop of blue.
I know you will notice me
So don't deny
As I wave by.

An End to Begin

The year tumbles
To a short day
Of huddle and scurry
The nights cold sweat
Beads the ground
Significant as prayer
The morning scream
That is winters song
Hangs on frozen staves
The carbon print
So sleeps in the breast
Of Mother's desire.

Printed in Great Britain
by Amazon